J
BIOG
FLACCO

Roberts, Russell,
1953-

Joe Flacco.

DATE			

6   JUN   2014

JOE FLACCO

Russell Roberts
with John Torres

Mitchell Lane
PUBLISHERS

P.O. Box 196
Hockessin, Delaware 19707
Visit us on the web: www.mitchelllane.com
Comments? Email us: mitchelllane@mitchelllane.com

Mitchell Lane
PUBLISHERS

Printing   1   2   3   4   5   6   7   8   9

A Robbie Reader Biography

Abigail Breslin
Adrian Peterson
Albert Einstein
Albert Pujols
Aly and AJ
Andrew Luck
AnnaSophia Robb
Ashley Tisdale
Brenda Song
Brittany Murphy
Buster Posey
Charles Schulz
Chris Johnson
Cliff Lee
Dale Earnhardt Jr.
David Archuleta
Demi Lovato
Donovan McNabb

Drake Bell & Josh Peck
Dr. Seuss
Dwayne "The Rock" Johnson
Dwyane Wade
Dylan & Cole Sprouse
Emily Osment
Hilary Duff
Jamie Lynn Spears
Jennette McCurdy
Jesse McCartney
Jimmie Johnson
Joe Flacco
Jonas Brothers
Keke Palmer
Larry Fitzgerald
LeBron James
Mia Hamm

Miguel Cabrera
Miley Cyrus
Miranda Cosgrove
Philo Farnsworth
Raven-Symoné
Robert Griffin III
Roy Halladay
Shaquille O'Neal
Story of Harley-Davidson
Sue Bird
Syd Hoff
Tiki Barber
Tim Lincecum
Tom Brady
Tony Hawk
Troy Polamalu
Victor Cruz
Victoria Justice

Library of Congress Cataloging-in-Publication Data
Roberts, Russell, 1953–
Joe Flacco / by Russell Roberts.
    pages cm. — (A Robbie reader)
Includes bibliographical references and index.
ISBN 978-1-61228-456-9 (library bound)
1. Flacco, Joe—Juvenile literature. 2. Football players—United States—Biography—Juvenile literature. I. Title.
GV939.F555R63 2014
796.332092—dc23
[B]
                                                                    2013027509
eBook ISBN: 9781612285164

ABOUT THE AUTHORS: Russell Roberts has written and published nearly 40 books for adults and children, including *C.C. Sabathia, Larry Fitzgerald, The Building of the Panama Canal, The Minotaur, The Battle of Waterloo, Ancient China, Scott Joplin,* and *The Railroad Fuels the Economy.* He lives in Bordentown, New Jersey, with his family and a fat, fuzzy, and crafty calico cat named Rusti.

John A. Torres is an award-winning sports columnist for *Florida Today* newspaper where he has covered professional and collegiate sports. John also covered the 2006 Olympics and has reported from many countries around the world. John is the author of more than 50 books, the majority of them about sports.

TABLE OF CONTENTS

Words in **bold** type can be found in the glossary.

Super Joe, quarterback Joe Flacco of the Baltimore Ravens, holds up the Vince Lombardi Trophy after leading the Ravens to a 34-31 victory over the San Francisco 49ers in Super Bowl XLVII.

MVP!

Baltimore Ravens quarterback Joe Flacco dropped back. The San Francisco 49ers defense rushed toward him. As calmly as if he was on the football field all alone, Flacco threw a rocket-fast pass to Ravens' wide receiver Anquan Boldin. Touchdown!

It was February 3, 2013. The Baltimore Ravens had just scored the first touchdown of Super Bowl XLVII. They went on to win the game 34-31. Flacco completed 22 of 33 passes for 287 yards and three touchdowns.

However, Flacco didn't just throw touchdown passes to help the Ravens win. Early in the third quarter the Ravens were ahead 28-6. It looked like it would be an easy victory. Then half of the lights in the Superdome went out! It took over 30 minutes for them to come back on. When they finally did, it was as if someone had recharged the 49ers too! They scored 17 straight points. Suddenly, the score was 28-23.

Flacco didn't panic. He led the Ravens to score two more field goals. It was enough to win.

Joe Flacco was named Most Valuable Player (MVP) of Super Bowl XLVII. "He . . . brought his team to a Super Bowl level,"

"You just won the Super Bowl; what are you going to do next?" Since 1987, winning Super Bowl players have been answering this famous question with, "I'm going to Disney World!" Joe Flacco celebrated his Super Bowl win with Mickey and Minnie in February 2013.

NFL Commissioner Roger Goodell told the Associated Press.

Before the 2012 football season, Flacco had taken a big chance. He turned down a **contract** offer from the Ravens. He was hoping to play well during the season so he would get a big contract at the end. Flacco told people that he was one of football's best quarterbacks. Some laughed.

During the season, Flacco was just ordinary. He threw 22 touchdown passes, had 10 interceptions and an 87.7 quarterback rating. But once the playoffs began, he turned into Super Joe. He threw for 1,140 yards and 11 touchdowns in four games. In a game the Ravens were losing to Denver, Flacco threw a 70-yard touchdown pass to Jacoby Jones as time was running out. Baltimore won the game in overtime. Some people say it was one of the greatest plays in NFL history.

Now he was a Super Bowl champion. "Unbelievable game," Flacco told the Associated Press about Super Bowl XLVII.

Nobody is laughing at what Joe Flacco says anymore.

Today, Joe plays football for the Baltimore Ravens, located just a few hours' drive from his hometown of Audubon, New Jersey. Joe got his start playing football there in seventh grade.

Growing Up

Southern New Jersey is much different from the northern part of the state. The north has big cities. The south is less crowded. It has farms where fruits and vegetables are grown.

Audubon is in southern New Jersey. There, Joseph Vincent Flacco was born on January 16, 1985. His parents, Steve and Karen, had known each other since high school. Both of them were athletes in college. Karen played basketball and softball at Trenton State College (now The College of New Jersey). Steve played football and baseball at the University of Pennsylvania. He had dreamed of being a **professional** baseball player.

Although Steve went to work in the **mortgage** business, he didn't forget about baseball. He put a batting cage in the back yard of his house. He thought Joe might play one day.

Joe grew rapidly. By the time he started high school he was six feet, two inches tall. He was the first in his family over six feet. The family marked the heights of Joe and his four

Family is very important to Joe, and he visits them often at their home in Audubon, New Jersey. The Flacco family, from left to right: Brian, Mike, Stephanie, Joe, Tom, John, Karen, and Steve.

younger brothers and younger sister on a green wall in their living room.

Joe started playing football in the seventh grade. He could throw the ball very far. However, the teams he played for already had their quarterbacks, so Joe played other positions. At Audubon High School he played football, baseball, and basketball. He won several honors and awards in football.

Joe's high school coach put together a tape of him playing football for colleges to watch. Suddenly colleges were trying to get Joe to come to their school. That's when Joe realized that he was a hot **prospect.**

When the University of Pittsburgh offered him a **scholarship,** he decided to go there. Little did he know how that decision would turn out.

Although Joe did see some playing time at the University of Pittsburgh, it wasn't very often. He hoped to transfer to the University of Delaware, but Joe was disappointed to find out that Pittsburgh wouldn't release him.

College Days

Joe played very little football during his time at the University of Pittsburgh. In 2003, his first year there, he was on the scout team, which is not the regular football team. The following year he completed just one pass for eleven yards.

Joe wanted to play more, so he decided to **transfer** to the University of Delaware. However, Pittsburgh would not release Joe to attend another school. He was forced to sit out the entire 2005 season.

In 2006 Joe finally got to be the starting quarterback for the Delaware Blue Hens. He started all 11 games and completed over 63 percent of his passes for 2,783 yards and 18 touchdowns. At six-foot-six, he was the tallest quarterback in school history.

The following year Joe was great. He earned All-American, All-East, All-Eastern College Athletic Conference, and All-Colonial

At the University of Delaware Joe blossomed into a star. His superb play made it likely that an NFL team would draft him when he became eligible to play professional ball.

Athletic Association honors. He completed 331 passes for 4,263 yards and 23 touchdowns. He led Delaware to the NCAA Division I Football Championship Subdivision national title game.

Although he set 20 records while at Delaware, Joe sometimes didn't realize what a great player he was. One day, he told Delaware football coach K. C. Keeler that he wanted to play baseball. Keeler told him that he was likely going to play professional football.

"I remember it like it was yesterday," Keeler told Delaware's student newspaper. "He said 'you think I am going to be a **draft** choice [of an NFL team]?' "

On the first day of the 2008 NFL draft, Keeler was proved right. Joe was picked by the Baltimore Ravens in the first round. He was the 18th player taken overall in the entire United States.

The NFL is much different from college. How would Joe do?

Initially, Joe wasn't supposed to play during his rookie year with the Ravens. But when Baltimore's other quarterbacks were injured, Joe became their starting quarterback. His performance that season led him to be named the Diet Pepsi Rookie of the Year.

Ravens Quarterback

Baltimore football fans have seen great quarterbacks. During the 1950s, '60s, and early '70s, fans watched Johnny Unitas quarterback the Baltimore Colts. He is one of the greatest quarterbacks in NFL history. He is still a Baltimore legend.

Joe would not have to worry about being compared to Unitas just yet. For the 2008 season, the Ravens wanted him to watch the games from the bench so he could learn as much as possible.

However, that plan quickly fell apart. The Ravens' two other quarterbacks got hurt during the preseason. Suddenly Joe Flacco was the starting quarterback.

Joe took right over. He led the Ravens to a record of 11-5. This was much better than the team's record the year before, when they were 5-11. Joe passed for 14 touchdowns. His fine play helped the team win a playoff spot. The Ravens won their first two playoff games before losing to Pittsburgh. Joe became the first

Joe and Head Coach John Harbaugh work very well together. This relationship between quarterback and coach is an important ingredient in their success.

rookie quarterback in NFL history to win two playoff games.

"I think Joe played like a **veteran,**" Ravens head coach John Harbaugh told the website NFLPlayers.com.

"Everyone else wants to say he was just a rookie," star linebacker Ray Lewis told NFLPlayers.com. "Joe, to me, is a very **mature** kid. He's a guy who understands the game of football."

To honor his great season, Joe was named the Diet Pepsi NFL Rookie of the Year.

In 2009, the Ravens dropped to 9-7. Joe improved his touchdown passes to 21. His quarterback rating bounced up nearly 10 points, to 88.9. The team still made the playoffs, where they won another game before losing. That made three playoff victories in two years for Joe.

What would happen next?

The job of an NFL quarterback is not an easy one. But Joe has proven that he can remain calm and throw accurate passes even as the opposing team's defense tries to stop him.

Top Quarterback

In 2010 Joe put it all together. He had the type of season that Ravens fans had been hoping for. He threw for 25 touchdowns with just 10 interceptions. His quarterback rating was an outstanding 93.6. The Ravens were one of the NFL's best football teams with a record of 12-4. But like before, they lost in the playoffs.

Joe slumped a bit in 2011. He passed for only 20 touchdowns, and his quarterback rating dropped to 80.9. Even with this performance, the Ravens finished 12-4 once again. And once again, they failed to reach the Super Bowl. Some people said it was Joe's fault.

Joe enjoys interacting with his fans, especially after a big victory like this one in January 2013. The Ravens had just won the AFC Championship Game against the New England Patriots and were now on their way to the Super Bowl.

He wasn't a top quarterback, they said. He was good, but not good enough.

Then came the 2012 season. Joe was determined to prove how good he was.

Joe has achieved great success on the football field. Yet he remains a quiet, almost shy person. He doesn't brag or show off. He goes

Although he's a star athlete, Joe gives willingly of his time to help those less fortunate. Here, he participates in the Polar Bear Plunge, where he jumps into icy cold water to raise money for the Special Olympics Maryland.

out to dinner with his family after every home game. He helps others. His life has been good, and he knows it.

"I am still playing a kids' game," he told the University of Delaware student newspaper.

When he's not playing football, he's very likely to be helping other people. One of his favorite causes is the Special Olympics Maryland. This organization provides sports training for children and adults with intellectual **disabilities.** The athletes also have the chance to compete. Joe participates in the annual Polar Bear Plunge by jumping into icy water to raise money for the program.

In addition to helping the Special Olympics, Joe has worked with the Ray Rice Day football clinic in New York, and he has helped to give out Thanksgiving turkeys to a poor Baltimore neighborhood. He has provided clothing for the homeless and participated in school fitness events.

Between charity and football, Joe has a full schedule. But he makes time for family, too.

On June 25, 2011, Joe married Dana Grady. She was his high school sweetheart. Almost exactly one year later, Dana gave birth to a baby boy. He was named Stephen, just like Joe's father. "My dad's my best friend," Joe said to *Baltimore Magazine*. After the Super Bowl, Joe said that they were expecting another child.

Football is only one part of Joe Flacco's life. In 2011, he married his high school sweetheart Dana.

Joe's teammates like and respect him. After the team beat New England to advance to the Super Bowl, Terrell Suggs shouted, "Joe Flacco, wherever you're going, I'm following you," a Yahoo Sports article reported.

"You give Joe time, he can beat anybody," said Ravens lineman Bryant McKinnie to Yahoo Sports.

Baltimore held a big parade to celebrate the Ravens' victory in Super Bowl XLVII, and of course Joe and his son Stephen were two of the guests of honor.

In 2013, Joe's earlier decision not to sign a contract paid off. After he led the Ravens to a Super Bowl win, the team offered Joe a new deal. This contract made him the highest-paid player in NFL history. The Ravens agreed to pay him $120.6 million over six years. Even though he is still young, Joe Flacco has proved he is one of the top quarterbacks in the NFL today.

It takes a lot of good players to win a Super Bowl. While Joe Flacco and the offense worked to score points, defensive players like linebacker Terrell Suggs worked to stop the opposing team from scoring.

27

CHRONOLOGY

1985   Born on January 16.

2003   Graduates from Audubon High School in Audubon, New Jersey; Enrolls at the University of Pittsburgh.

2005   Transfers to the University of Delaware.

2007   As a senior, earns All-American, All-East, All-ECAC, and All-CAA honors.

2008   Drafted by the Baltimore Ravens on April 26. Signs a five-year, $30 million contract.

2011   Marries high school sweetheart Dana Grady.

2012   Son Stephen is born.

2013   Leads the Baltimore Ravens to a Super Bowl win; Signs a six-year, $120.6 million contract, making him the highest-paid NFL player to date.

CAREER STATISTICS

Year	Team	Games	PC	PA	C%	Yards	LPC	TDs	INTs	R
2008	Baltimore	16	257	428	60	2971	70 yards	14	12	80.3
2009	Baltimore	16	315	499	63.1	3613	72 yards	21	12	88.9
2010	Baltimore	16	306	489	62.6	3622	67 yards	25	10	93.6
2011	Baltimore	16	312	542	57.6	3610	74 yards	20	12	80.9
2012	Baltimore	16	317	531	59.7	3817	61 yards	22	10	87.7

PC = Pass Completions, PA = Pass Attempts, C% = Completion Percentage, LPC = Longest Pass Completed, TDs = Touchdowns, INTs = Interceptions, R = Rating

FIND OUT MORE

Books

Kelley, K. C. *Quarterbacks.* New York: Gareth Stevens, 2009.

Krumenauer, Heidi. *Joe Flacco.* Hockessin, DE: Mitchell Lane Publishers, 2010.

Sandler, Michael. *Joe Flacco and the Baltimore Ravens: Super Bowl XLVII.* New York: Bearport Publishing, 2014.

Sandler, Michael. *Pro Football's Most Spectacular Quarterbacks.* New York: Bearport Publishing, 2011.

Works Consulted

Baltimore Ravens. *Player Roster.* "Joe Flacco." January 2013. http://www.baltimoreravens.com/team/roster/joe-flacco/3e20766f-6520-4ca1-9901-44389aaea8b8/

Battista, Judy. "Measuring Up, On the Doorway and On the Draft Board." *The New York Times,* April 24, 2008. http://www.nytimes.com/2008/04/24/sports/football/24flacco.html?pagewanted=all&_r=0

Benjamin, Amalie. "Not Your Average Joe." *The Boston Globe,* January 21, 2012. http://www.boston.com/sports/football/patriots/articles/2012/01/21/joe_flacco_is_ready_to_get_past_the_questions/

Cole, Jason. "Maybe Now Observers Will Label Super Bowl-Bound Joe Flacco an Elite NFL Quarterback." Yahoo Sports, January 21, 2013. http://sports.yahoo.com/news/nfl--maybe-now-observers-will-consider-super-bowl-bound-joe-flacco-an-elite-nfl-quarterback-071137436.html

Ginsburg, David. "Flacco Begins Collecting Awards As Super Bowl MVP." Associated Press, February 4, 2013.

Klemko, Robert. "'General' Joe Flacco Keeps Cool Ahead of AFC Title Game." *USA Today,* January 19, 2013. http://www.usatoday.com/story/sports/nfl/2013/01/18/ravens-joe-flacco-keeps-cool-afc-championship-patriots/1846703/

Maaddi, Rob. "Joe Flacco: A Blue Hen With a Golden Arm." Associated Press, January 25, 2013.

FIND OUT MORE

McInerney, Daniel. "Flacco Five Years After Delaware." *The Review,* December 3, 2012. http://www.udreview.com/sports/flacco-five-years-after-delaware-1.2963347#.UbjTcEDvu8A

NFL.com: "Joe Flacco." 2013. http://nfl.com/player/joeflacco/382/careerstats

Reeves, Barry, and Ron Smith, eds., *Sporting News Selects Pro Football's Greatest Quarterbacks.* St. Louis, MO: The Sporting News, 2005.

Schwab, Frank. "Joe Flacco Validates Himself With a Super Bowl MVP Award." Yahoo Sports, February 3, 2013. http://sports.yahoo.com/blogs/nfl-shutdown-corner/joe-flacco-validates-himself-super-bowl-mvp-award-035953835--nfl.html

Unger, Mike. "Joe Knows." *Baltimore Magazine,* November 2012. http://www.baltimoremagazine.net/people/2012/11/joe-flacco-ravens-joe-knows

Wilson, Aaron. "Flacco Showed No Rookie Learning Curve in 2008." NFLPlayers.com, June 16, 2009. https://www.nflplayers.com/Articles/Player-Profile/Flacco-Showed-No-Rookie-Learning-Curve-in-2008/

Wilt, Zach. "Joe Flacco Has the Best Postseason Road Record in NFL History." *Baltimore Sports Report,* January 21, 2013. http://baltimoresportsreport.com/joe-flacco-afc-championship-36871.html

On the Internet

Baltimore Ravens: Ravens Rookies Kids Club
http://www.baltimoreravens.com/ravenstown/rookies-kids-club.html

NFL Rush
http://www.nflrush.com/

Official Website of Joe Flacco
http://www.joeflacco5.com/

University of Delaware Athletics
http://www.bluehens.com/#

GLOSSARY

contract (KON-trakt)—An agreement between two or more parties to do something.

disability (dis-uh-BIL-i-tee)—Lack of adequate physical or mental ability.

draft (DRAFT)—A selection of new players.

mature (muh-TOOR)—Complete in growth or development.

mortgage (MAWR-gij)—A loan given for the purchase of real estate.

professional (pruh-FESH-uh-nl)—Pursuing an occupation as a way of making a living.

prospect (PROS-pekt)—A potential or likely candidate.

rookie (ROOK-ee)—An athlete playing his or her first season.

scholarship (SKOL-er-ship)—Money given to a student to be used towards schooling.

transfer (TRANS-fer)—To withdraw from one school and enter another.

veteran (VET-er-uhn)—A person with a lot of experience.

PHOTO CREDITS: Cover, p. 1—Rich Schultz/Getty Images; p. 4—Patrick Semansky/AP Photo; p. 6—Matt Stroshane/Disney Parks/Getty Images; p. 8— Patrick Semansky/AP Photo; p. 10—Jeff Fusco/Reebook/Getty Images;p. 12—Sean Brady/WireImage; p. 14—Joe Giblin/AP Photo; p. 16—Paul Spinelli/AP Photo; p. 18— Gene Puskar/AP Photo; p. 20—Paul Spinelli/AP Photo; p. 22—Jim Davis/The Boston Globe/Getty Images; p. 23—Ann Heisenfelt/AP Photo; p. 25—Andrew Toth/Starpix/AP Photo; p. 26—Steve Ruark/AP Photo; p. 27—Greg Trott/AP Photo. Every effort has been made to locate all copyright holders of materials used in this book. Any errors or omissions will be corrected in future editions of the book.

INDEX